The Word Wizard's Book of ADVERBS

Robin Johnson

Crabtree
Publishing
Company

www.crabtreebooks.com

Author
Robin Johnson

Publishing plan research and development
Reagan Miller, Crabtree Publishing Company

Editorial director
Kathy Middleton

Project coordinator
Kelly Spence

Editor
Anastasia Suen

Proofreader and indexer
Wendy Scavuzzo

Photo research
Robin Johnson, Katherine Berti

Design & prepress
Katherine Berti

Print coordinator
Katherine Berti

Photographs
Shutterstock: © Beelde Photography: p15
All other images from Shutterstock

Library and Archives Canada Cataloguing in Publication

Johnson, Robin (Robin R.), author
       The word wizard's book of adverbs / Robin Johnson.

(Word wizard)
Includes index.
Issued in print and electronic formats.
ISBN 978-0-7787-1306-7 (bound).--ISBN 978-0-7787-1314-2 (pbk.).--
ISBN 978-1-4271-7763-6 (pdf).--ISBN 978-1-4271-7759-9 (html)

       1. English language--Adverb--Juvenile literature. I. Title.

PE1325.J64 2014   j428.2   C2014-903815-1
                                                 C2014-903816-X

Library of Congress Cataloging-in-Publication Data

Johnson, Robin (Robin R.) author.
 The Word Wizard's book of adverbs / Robin Johnson.
     p. cm. -- (Word Wizard)
 Includes index.
 ISBN 978-0-7787-1306-7 (reinforced library binding) --
 ISBN 978-0-7787-1314-2 (pbk.) -- ISBN 978-1-4271-7763-6 (electronic pdf) --
 ISBN 978-1-4271-7759-9 (electronic html)
 1. English language--Adverb--Juvenile literature. 2. English language--
 Parts of speech--Juvenile literature. I. Title. II. Title: Book of adverbs.

 PE1325.J66 2014
 425'.76--dc23
                                    2014029993

Crabtree Publishing Company

www.crabtreebooks.com   1-800-387-7650

Printed in the U.S.A./092014/JA20140811

Published in Canada
Crabtree Publishing
616 Welland Ave.
St. Catharines, Ontario
L2M 5V6

Published in the United States
Crabtree Publishing
PMB 59051
350 Fifth Avenue, 59th Floor
New York, New York 10118

Published in the United Kingdom
Crabtree Publishing
Maritime House
Basin Road North, Hove
BN41 1WR

Published in Australia
Crabtree Publishing
3 Charles Street
Coburg North
VIC 3058

Contents

Magic words

Words work magically! They let us dream big and go far. They help us sing sweetly. They make us laugh hard. Words started our stories once upon a time. And they let us live happily ever after. We can do so much with words!

Words make the world go around!

Magic moves

We use words to tell stories now and then. We use words to ask questions clearly. We use words to find answers quickly. We use words called **adverbs**. Adverbs describe how things move.

The Word Wizards know some magic moves. But they need your help to learn about adverbs.

Words can even move you upside down!

What are adverbs?

Adverbs are words that describe **verbs**. Verbs tell what people or things are doing. The word "jump" is a verb.

Adverbs tell us more about verbs. They tell how, when, or where actions take place. The words "wildly," "soon," and "around" are adverbs. We could use those adverbs to describe jumping.

Adverbs tell how

Some adverbs tell how things happen. We say, "The boy jumps joyfully. He leaps high in the air." The words "joyfully" and "high" are adverbs. They describe how the boy moves. How do you move?

Word Wizard in training

Help the Word Wizard find the adverbs below. Do they tell how, when, or where actions happen?

This girl is bouncing *up* and *down.*

These girls are laughing *hard.* They are really having a ball!

Adverbs tell when

Some adverbs tell when actions take place. What are you doing today? You are reading this book now! The words "today" and "now" are adverbs. They tell that actions happen in the present.

Before and after

Some adverbs tell that actions have already taken place. "Before" and "yesterday" describe actions in the past. Other adverbs tell that actions will take place. "After" and "tomorrow" describe actions in the future.

This girl is reading a book now, too. She is learning all about adverbs!

Word Wizard in training

It is time to help the Word Wizard! Which caption tells when actions take place? Find it now!

These kids are ready to get the ball rolling!

These kids are already playing soccer.

9

Adverbs tell where

Some adverbs tell where actions take place. You can go here or there. You can play inside or outside. You can clean upstairs or downstairs. You can bike near or far. You can do things anywhere! These place words are all adverbs.

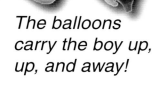

The balloons carry the boy up, up, and away!

Word Wizard in training

Adverbs help us get where we want to go. Turn left. Turn right. Go straight. Turn around. Go back. We would be lost without adverbs!

Look at the maze below. Can you help the Word Wizard get home? Use adverbs to tell her the way.

Sentences

We join words to form **sentences**. Sentences are complete thoughts or ideas. They are made up of many kinds of words. Each word has a job to do. Adverbs give us details about verbs in sentences. They tell how, when, and where actions happen.

How do these animals move? Use adverbs in a sentence to describe each animal's action.

This girl and her dog are dressed alike. They are both super!

Finding adverbs

Adverbs can come before verbs in sentences. We say, "My pet bunny always hops." Adverbs can also come after verbs. We say, "My bird chirps loudly." Some adverbs are easy to spot in sentences. They end in the **suffix** "ly." Suffixes are letters added to the end of words. They change the meaning of the words.

Uh-oh! The cat chased the dog around. They accidentally broke the pot!

Adverbs compare

We can use adverbs to **compare** actions. Comparing means telling what is the same or different. To compare two actions, we add the suffix "er." We say the yellow apple grows big. The green cabbage grows bigger. To compare more actions, we add the suffix "est." The orange pumpkin grows biggest of all!

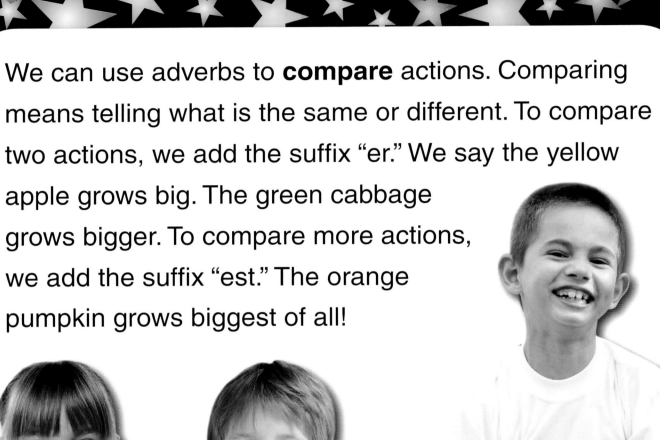

Race cars zoom fast around the track!

Which car moves most slowly around the track? Which moves most quickly?

More or less

Adverbs that end in "ly" follow a different rule. We add "more" or "less" to compare two actions. The red car moves more quickly than the green car. The green car moves less quickly.

We add "most" or "least" to compare more than two actions. The white car moves least quickly. It loses the race. The blue car moves most quickly. It wins the race!

Adjectives to adverbs

Some **adjectives** can magically become adverbs! Adjectives are words that describe people, places, and things. We can say, "The boy plays loud music." The word "loud" is an adjective. It describes the music. We can also say, "The boy plays his music loudly." The word "loudly" is an adverb. It describes the verb "plays."

This girl has a happy smile. She is smiling happily.

Forming adverbs

We form some adverbs by adding "ly." The adjective "bad" becomes the adverb "badly." The adjective "nice" becomes the adverb "nicely." Some words follow different rules.

Adjective ends in	Example	Rule	Adverb formed
a **consonant** then the letter "y"	scary	change "y" to "i" before adding "ly"	scarily
	noisy		noisily
	easy		easily
	crazy		crazily
a **vowel** then the letter "l"	careful	keep the "l" and add "ly"	carefully
	loyal		loyally
	cruel		cruelly
	awful		awfully

Vowels are the alphabet letters a, e, i, o, u, and sometimes y. Consonants are the other alphabet letters.

Sometimes y is a consonant, and sometimes y is a vowel.

Adverbs add details

Adverbs add important details to our stories. They help us **communicate** with others. To communicate means to share ideas and information. We choose the adverbs that tell our stories best. We use different adverbs to keep our stories interesting.

Synonyms

Some adverbs are **synonyms**. Synonyms mean the same thing or nearly the same thing as other words. The words "happily" and "gladly" are synonyms. The words "bravely" and "boldly" are synonyms. They are words with the same meanings.

Word Wizard in training

Use your finger to match up these synonyms. Think hard and match them carefully!

kindly	beautifully
silently	quietly
nearly	gently
prettily	joyfully
happily	almost
softly	nicely

Adverbs give clues

Adverbs give us clues when we read stories. They tell us more about the **characters**. Characters are the people and animals in books. We cannot see how, when, or where they move. So we check adverbs for clues. Then we paint pictures of them in our heads.

Talk about adverbs

Adverbs also tell us how characters feel. We look for clues in their **dialogue**. Dialogue is the things characters say. Adverbs tell us how characters say them. If a character talks excitedly, how do they feel? If a character speaks shyly, how do they feel?

Adverbs make stories come alive!

How are these birds talking? Use adverbs to describe them.

Word Wizard in training

Help the Word Wizard find the adverbs below. They will tell you how the people feel. Then read the sentences aloud. Use your voice to show their feelings.

"We won first prize," the students said *proudly.*

"I dropped my ice-cream cone," the girl said *sadly.*

Write on!

Now it is time to make your own story!
Get some paper and crayons. Then
draw a character. You can make up one.
You can draw one you already know.
You can even draw the Word Wizard!

Add a sentence to your story. Use adverbs to tell how,
when, or where the character moves. Now add a
sentence of dialogue. What does your character say?
How do they say it? Use adverbs to paint a picture
and tell your story.

Learning more

Books

Adverbs (Grammar Basics) by Kate Riggs. Creative Paperbacks, 2013.

Doggie Day Camp: Verb and Adverb Adventures by Cynthia Reeg. Guardian Angel Publishing Inc., 2008.

Hole-in-One Adverbs (Grammar All-Stars) by Doris Fisher. Gareth Stevens Publishing, 2008.

Lazily, Crazily, Just a Bit Nasally: More about Adverbs (Words Are CATegorical) by Brian P. Cleary. First Avenue Editions, 2010.

Websites

Shoot adverbs with an owl cannon in this fun game.
www.turtlediary.com/grade-3-games/ela-games/precision-adverb.html

Choose your words carefully in this adverb matching game.
www.oswego.org/ocsd-web/match/term/matchgeneric2.asp?filename=msmith5adverbmatch

Test your knowledge with this adverb quiz.
http://quizzes.cc/the-adverb-quiz-242

Match and learn adverbs at this fun web page.
www.learnenglish.de/Games/Adverbs/Adverbs.html

Words to know

adjective (AJ-ik-tiv) A word that describes a person, place, or thing

adverb (AD-vurb) A word that tells how, when, or where an action takes place

character (KAR-ik-ter) A person or animal in a book

communicate (kuh-MYOO-ni-keyt) To share ideas and information

compare (kuhm-PAIR) To tell what is the same or different

consonant (KON-suh-nuhnt) A letter of the alphabet that is not a vowel

dialogue (DAHY-uh-lawg) The things characters in books say

sentence (SEN-tns) A complete thought or idea

suffix (SUHF-iks) One or more letters added to the end of a word

synonym (SIN-uh-nim) A word that means the same thing or nearly the same thing as another word

verb (vurb) An action word that tells what a person or thing is doing

vowel (VOU-uhl) The alphabet letters a, e, i, o, u, or y

Index